Contents

I0428392

Acknowledgements iii

Introduction 1

Executive Summary 3

City Summaries 9

    Boston, Massachusetts 11

    Burnsville, Minnesota 15

    El Paso, Texas 19

    New Brighton, Minnesota 25

    New Haven, Connecticut 31

    Sallisaw, Oklahoma 35

    San José, California 39

More City Examples 43

Additional Resources 57

About This Report 69

Acknowledgements

N LC's Institute for Youth, Education, and Families (YEF Institute) would like to thank the members of municipal and law enforcement staff from cities across the nation who shared their knowledge and experience for this publication.

In addition, the YEF Institute is indebted to two dedicated individuals for their strong commitment to the project and consistently helpful guidance and advice during its implementation: Katherine McQuay, senior policy analyst in the Office of Community Oriented Policing Services at the U.S. Department of Justice, and John Firman, director of research for the International Association of Chiefs of Police (IACP). Without their assistance, this report would not have been possible.

John Calhoun, former president and chief executive officer of the National Crime Prevention Council and senior consultant to the YEF Institute, crafted the original vision for the project and provided overall guidance and direction throughout its various stages. He and senior consultant Andrew O. Moore conducted interviews with city leaders and prepared the written profiles of each city's efforts.

Numerous NLC staff also played important roles in the research and publication of this report. Clifford M. Johnson, the YEF Institute's executive director, and Leon T. Andrews, program director for youth development, helped coordinate various aspects of the project and provided overall editorial direction and support. Jessica Sandoval and Melissa Rogers conducted interviews with city leaders and led the early phases of NLC's research and data collection efforts, and Colleen McCarthy verified information of the organizations included in the Resources section and provided staff support during preparation of the final manuscript. Michael Karpman offered additional editorial support, and Susan Gamble was responsible for the report's design and layout.

Special thanks to members of NLC's Advisory Group on Mayor / Law Enforcement Partnerships, including:

Sheila Allen Bell, Administrator, Community Services Department, City of New Haven, Connecticut

Robert A. Bermingham, Jr., Coordinator, Fairfax County Coordinating Council on Gang Prevention, Fairfax, Virginia

Donald Bridges, Region 2 Director and Treasurer, National Association of School Resource Officers, St. Paul, Minnesota

Chief David E. Dial, Vice-Chair, IACP Community Policing Committee, Naperville, Illinois

Brenda Donald Walker, Deputy Mayor, Children, Youth, Families, and Elders, Washington, D.C.

The Honorable William D. Euille, Mayor, City of Alexandria, Virginia

John Firman, Director of Research, International Association of Chiefs of Police, Alexandria, Virginia

George George, Assistant Principal, Our Lady of Sorrows Catholic School, Takoma Park, Maryland

Christen Gutierrez, Student, Our Lady of Sorrows Catholic School, Takoma Park, Maryland

Ashley Hawkins, Student, Our Lady of Sorrows Catholic School, Takoma Park, Maryland

The Honorable Daun S. Hester, 2006 Chair, NLC's Council on Youth, Education, and Families and Councilmember, City of Norfolk, Virginia

The Honorable Charles Hughes, Council President, City of Gary, Indiana

David Kass, Executive Director, Fight Crime: Invest in Kids, Washington, D.C.

Thomas MacLellan, Policy Analyst, Criminal Justice, Center for Best Practices, National Governor's Association, Washington, D.C.

Chief J. Thomas Manger, Montgomery County Police Department, Rockville, Maryland

The Honorable Stephen Rideout, Former Chief Judge, Alexandria Juvenile and Domestic Relations, District Court, Alexandria, Virginia

Chief Charles E. Samarra, Alexandria Police Department, Alexandria, Virginia

Anthony J. Schembri, 2006 Chair, IACP Juvenile Justice Committee and Secretary, Florida Department of Juvenile Justice, Tallahassee, Florida

Chief Steven J. White, Former Chair, IACP Juvenile Justice Committee, Doylestown, Pennsylvania

D ear Municipal Leader:

Without question, mayors, police chiefs, and other municipal officials are essential leaders of strong and effective initiatives to improve the safety and well-being of children and youth. City leaders have an unrivalled ability to focus attention on an issue, convene key stakeholders and insist they work together, connect with residents at the neighborhood level, carry out the vision, and ensure a focus on results. This document presents numerous inspiring examples in which teams led by mayors, law enforcement, and other city officials have achieved the universally-shared goal of greater safety and improved life chances for young people in their communities.

This publication is for you — for mayors, city managers, police chiefs, and other municipal leaders who are in the trenches of the ongoing fight to protect our nation's children and youth. It will also be helpful to you if you work with such leaders on a regular basis and want to enlist their help in efforts to keep young people safe — a top priority for cities across America.

The National League of Cities' Institute for Youth, Education, and Families, with support and assistance from the U.S. Department of Justice Office of Community Oriented Policing Services and the International Association of Chiefs of Police, produced this report to describe efforts of mayors and police executives to work together to promote the safety and well-being of children and youth. You will find tips, motivating examples, and practical action steps that you can apply in your own city or town. You will also draw inspiration from locally-tested and endorsed strategies. For NLC, it is indeed inspiring to:

- Find descriptions of police who balance enforcement with compassion in how they respond to the needs of children.

- See that the right leadership, resources, and community-level drive can knit together seemingly diffuse efforts into broad, high-impact strategies, which in turn can be borrowed and adapted by others.

- Have a store of ideas upon which to build locally.

- Gain further evidence of the effectiveness of cross-system collaboration.

- Know that it is possible to move from a focus on programs to an overall shift in how cities and police departments do business.

The National League of Cities remains committed to supporting municipal initiatives that improve the safety and well-being of our next generation. We hope that the examples in this report will enable you and others in your community to bring new energy and ideas to this effort.

Donald J. Borut
Executive Director
National League of Cities

Clifford M. Johnson, Executive Director
Institute for Youth, Education, and Families
National League of Cities

Executive Summary

T hrough effective partnerships among mayors, police chiefs, and munic- ipal agencies, cities and towns across America have enhanced the safety and well-being of children and youth. The initiatives profiled in this report address a broad range of concerns, but they share four critical elements: the belief that collaboration is essential for achieving results; a commitment to community oriented policing strategies on a citywide basis or in targeted neighborhoods; a focus on key indicators to preserve momentum and measure progress; and efforts to craft a shared community vision that can sustain these partnerships over time. Each initiative in its own way has played an important role in protecting and nurturing the next generation.

Forging Collaborations Between Mayors and Law Enforcement Leaders

Municipal partnerships are launched for many different reasons, but the catalyst that brings mayors, police chiefs, and other city agencies together often is the recognition that neither the city nor its young people can thrive without such collaborative efforts. In New Haven, Connecticut, the mayor and police chief responded to concerns about the effects of street violence on children. In Boston, Massachusetts, and New Brighton, Minnesota, the inspiration for cities arose from one or more neighborhoods where violent crimes were most likely to occur. And in still other cities, the motivation to act grew out of a desire to prevent potential problems (e.g., Chula Vista, California's launch of the Olweus bullying prevention program or Sallisaw, Oklahoma's adaptation of school-based substance abuse prevention strate- gies) or to continue building on progress (e.g., the aspirations of Sheboygan, Wisconsin, and Fort Worth, Texas, to earn a top ranking as the safest city in the nation).

The strongest approaches also reflect an awareness among top officials that "we can't do it alone" — that city, law enforcement, and community leaders need each other's sustained help and participation to ensure the safety and well-being of children and youth. In effective municipal partnerships, mayors and police chiefs act in concert, successfully developing and pursuing a coordinated strategy that pulls together the resources of law enforcement and other city and community agencies.

As a partnership gathers momentum, it becomes clearer that sustaining it is the responsibility of the entire community, not just one agency. The very broad participation in El Paso's Youth Initiative Program exemplifies this recognition. As roles blur and blend, new voices emerge to advocate for children's safety. One Boston police lieutenant on the gang unit now says, "These are not bad kids. They need education and jobs. Jail won't help them." And in New Haven, child development is a subject now taught at the police academy.

Combining Citywide Approaches with Targeted Initiatives

The various city strategies highlighted in this report are all anchored in community oriented policing, defined and adapted locally in response to community culture and needs. Within this context, however, both citywide strategies and initiatives that target specific areas or neighborhoods can play critical roles in enhancing the safety and well-being of children and youth. El Paso, Texas, San José, California, and other cities have adopted comprehensive strategies that reach across the entire jurisdiction. These strategies blend prevention, intervention, and enforcement, and find ways to "transmit" the moral voice of the community as well. Goals here are broad and visionary. Local officials speak of "a city free of gangs and crime" that "helps young people realize hopes and dreams" in order to build "successful and productive schools, homes, and neighborhoods."

Other strategies focus on reclaiming a violence-plagued section of the city — from an apartment complex in New Brighton to targeted neighborhoods in Boston and Philadelphia. Many start with children and young adolescents who are still in school. Others, as in Providence, Rhode Island, work to re-integrate former prisoners upon their return to the community. A host of efforts intriguingly blend prevention, support, and enforcement where clergy and police make joint home visits and work together to broker access to children's and family services. Still other cities have broken new ground in the design and application of familiar assets such as police athletic leagues and school resource officers.

As mayor-law enforcement partnerships strengthen community oriented policing, key partners then take steps to form a coalition that reaches horizontally across city agencies and extends vertically to involve professionals and community leaders from various systems, services, and sectors. City and police officials often look beyond their communities as well, connecting county and state resources to the coalition efforts.

Using Data to Sustain Momentum and Measure Progress

A key to sustaining momentum lies in collecting and publicizing data that allows everyone to measure progress over time. Cities measure progress and proclaim success based on outcome measures as well as process measures or "outputs." Both can be important to telling the story and continuously building support for city-police partnerships. Whether focusing on a reduction in crime rates (El Paso), less bullying (Chula Vista), lower rates of domestic violence (New Haven), or a decline in recidivism (Boston), cities have chosen high-impact outcomes to pursue. Changes in public perceptions have also proven important in some cities — Sheboygan's efforts have led to a drop in community fear, New Brighton's to higher citizen satisfaction with police.

The range of process measures that cities can track and report is quite broad. El Paso and other cities note the rise in the number of participants in youth programs; other cities note up-ticks in the number of citizen volunteers. Increased use of public spaces gets counted in several cities. Boston and other cities that have adapted the Operation Homefront approach track the growing number of home visits by clergy and police.

Ensuring Sustainability and Reaffirming a Shared Community Vision

Effective leadership is about more than funding or operating programs. It is also about defining or reaffirming and giving voice to community norms and aspirations. Mayors and police chiefs can convey the moral imperative, and in some cases the outrage, that creates a sense of urgency and citywide commitment to improve the safety and well-being of children and youth. In addition, sustaining municipal partnerships is an ever-present challenge that requires repeated efforts to bring people to — and keep them at — the table. Strong and clear invitations by city, law enforcement, and community leaders bring people together, and active participation by the mayor and police chief in particular keep partners coming back.

Cities and towns have also succeeded in sustaining partnership efforts by widening their scope just enough to appeal to multiple interests and concerns. For instance, Worcester's Youth Mentoring Program and Tupelo's Police Athletic League center seek to improve and protect both the safety and the well-being of children and youth. This slightly broader framing takes the city, police, and their partners out of a purely defensive role and enables the community to coalesce around a positive agenda, one that emphasizes nurturing and positive youth development while blending protection, prevention, and intervention strategies.

Securing long-term funding sources is another key to sustainability. Cities have often started by redeploying city funds or securing a state or federal grant. Again, leadership from the top plays a critical role. The mayor and police chief can signal that the safety and well-being of children and youth are top priorities by convening a task force, naming and recognizing its members, and working with the task force early on to develop a financing strategy for the initiative. Staff support for this group from a municipal agency or community-based intermediary will also increase the odds for long-term success.

Building upon these initial steps, cities can tackle the more complex challenges of establishing communications strategies, building infrastructure, promoting community involvement and buy-in, gathering information, and engaging youth, parents, and other residents. The municipal partnerships profiled in this report provide helpful guidance for cities in these and other key areas.

∼

Ten Ideas for Getting Started

1. Set goals for child safety and well-being in the mayor's annual state of the city address.

2. Survey people who will benefit from programs/initiatives.

3. Develop memoranda of understanding to begin sharing data.

4. Highlight the costs of doing nothing.

5. Hold small-scale, monthly "meet your mayor and police chief" breakfasts or lunches, or regular public meetings.

6. Have the mayor and chief of police meet one-on-one regularly to discuss the safety of children, youth, and families.

7. Sign up "unusual suspects" as partners (e.g., a public health officer or commissioner).

8. Direct one or more city agencies and the police department to collaboratively develop and submit a funding proposal.

9. Get young people involved in planning, implementation, and evaluation.

10. Close ineffective programs.

Adapted from discussions of NLC's Advisory Group on Mayor / Law Enforcement Partnerships, June 2006

City Summaries

This section highlights the efforts of seven cities to create mayor-law enforcement partnerships that promote the safety and well-being of children and youth. Each city summary examines the motivation of the city to focus on children and youth; describes the decision to create a partnership as a strategic response; summarizes the steps taken in the partnership and the accomplishments to date; identifies the appropriate goals and measurements of success; and reflects on aspects of its efforts that could be replicated by other cities.

Boston, Massachusetts

(pop. 559,034)

Boston's Ceasefire strategy is by now well-known. This partnership of law enforcement, service providers, and other community leaders articulates clear, direct norms and messages that violence will not be tolerated and that services and alternatives are available to those most likely to become offenders and victims of violence. Ceasefire involves a quick response by police to flare-ups of firearm violence based on shared intelligence, direct communication with gang members to let them know that violence will bring intensive law enforcement attention combined with an offer of help, a focus on prosecuting the most dangerous offenders, and disruption of the flow of arms to gangs.

In the early 1990s, with roughly 30 percent of the 150 homicides per year taking the lives of young people, Boston seemed truly out of control. Children and youth were avoiding school and staying home. Among 10 cities it surveyed, the Centers for Disease Control gave Boston the highest score on its fear scale. A shoot-out in a local church over the casket of a teen victim of gun violence during a funeral service brought the simmering issue to a public boil. The community, led in this case by local ministers, met with Mayor

11

Thomas Menino and then-Chief of Police Paul Evans. Something had to be done now and that "something" would require the energy of everybody. In this cauldron, Ceasefire, which led to what is now called the "Boston Miracle," was forged.

Ceasefire's core elements include a detailed analysis of where the violence is and who is perpetrating it, an intense communication effort to current and potential troublemakers that the consequences of violent acts will be swift and serious, comprehensive help and service provision to at-risk youth and their families, and the voice of the community clearly expressing its balanced norm of intervention and enforcement that "we will not tolerate violence here and we stand ready to help."

It worked. For two years in the mid-1990s, Boston recorded no youth homicides. It was indeed a "miracle" that was adopted as a strategy by many jurisdictions across the country.

As the city witnessed the success of a dramatic reduction in crime, changes in project leadership, and shifting municipal priorities, homicide rates again began to increase. The city recently committed itself to reviving Ceasefire, and has launched innovative companion efforts for serving youth based on Ceasefire's strategic foundation, such as Operation Homefront, the Boston Reentry Initiative, and the Violent Offender Reentry Program.

Operation Homefront, which began as an informal arrangement between police and clergy to visit the homes of troubled juveniles together, has become formalized. School police officers and administration officials iden-tify schools with trouble brewing. Anti-violence presentations are made in those schools to the entire student body. Joint visits are scheduled by police and clergy to the homes of troubled students needing individual attention. Services, both educational and social, are offered to parents and children to assist in problem-solving. Family visits are followed up by calls, letters, or additional visits.

Homefront's goals combine a promise of safety with a promise of support for the future: "To reduce violence in the Boston Public Schools and…in neighborhoods…to ensure the safety and security of each student attending Boston's schools and in their neighborhoods…to provide families the support they need to ensure their children's success in school and life…" (from the Boston Police Department's description of Operation Homefront).

While outcome measures are not available, process measures — the number of visits, school presentations, and follow-up services provided — are impressive. Support from the mayor was essential. According to Jen Maconochie, director of strategic planning for the Police Department, "Mayor Menino helped the schools and police get together. He also involved his Department for Youth and Families as well as [the Departments of] Public Health and Parks and Recreation. We could not have done it without his support."

Recognizing that much of the increase in violent crime could be attributed to former offenders returning to their communities from jail or prison, the city created the Boston Reentry Initiative (BRI). Its strategic core parallels Ceasefire: focus on enforcement and assistance for the most serious returning offenders and ensure that the community's voice is heard. While BRI focuses on adult inmates, most of them between the ages of 18-32, a companion effort, the Serious and Violent Offender Reentry Program, has been started in the Massachusetts Department of Youth Services (DYS). Tina Saetti, who designed and started the program, says, "Know that we don't take creampuffs. We focus on the worst of the worst, the 'impact players,' gang members, those in for attempted murder, carjacking, firearm possession, those who hurt the community most. We screen for trouble. The results? A 25% recidivism rate compared to 46% for DYS as a whole."

Although the proportions may differ, Ceasefire, Operation Homefront, BRI, and the Violent Offender Reentry Program share the same core elements: enforcement, prevention, provision of services, and a clear message from municipal and community leaders that "the violence must stop, and we are here to help."

Contact:

Blake Norton, Director of Public Affairs and Community Programs
Office of the Police Commissioner
Boston Police Department
One Schroeder Plaza
Boston, MA 02120-2014
(617) 343-4500
NortonB.bpd@ci.boston.ma.us

Leadership Keys

◉ **Communicated a unified message that balances prevention, intervention, enforcement, and community voice.**

City leaders and their community partners simultaneously offered support services to at-risk youth and violent offenders while emphasizing the consequences of criminal behavior. Key stakeholders transmitted this message through schools, churches, home visits, and other interactions with service providers, law enforcement officials, and community members. The dual focus on enforcement and assistance to young people dramatically reduced homicide rates and recidivism.

◉ **Used leadership roles to strengthen a collaborative approach.**

The mayor and chief of police were both instrumental in fostering a collaborative environment that tapped the strengths of diverse public agencies and nonprofit organizations. Each agency or group at the table offered a unique asset: the ability to reach young people through the schools, connect youth with services, reinforce community norms and morals, or instill a sense of safety. The mayor repeatedly used his leadership position to convene these partners and sustain the momentum over time.

◉ **Implemented a highly effective community oriented policing strategy.**

Boston's community-oriented approach led to improved law enforcement and greater success in preventing violence. For instance, by participating in joint home visits with local clergy, police officers forged stronger connections with residents, delivered a credible message of support and enforcement to youth, and targeted young people who were at greatest risk.

Burnsville, Minnesota

(pop. 59,159)

Centrally located across from the police station in Burnsville, Minnesota, a Twin Cities suburb, THE GARAGE is a supervised city recreation and entertainment center heavily used by area teens and supported by many community institutions. THE GARAGE had its start in July 1999 as the old garage for city vehicles, and since then has grown into a community. Now young people develop and drive a broad and vibrant range of programs at THE GARAGE, in cooperation with adults ranging from recreation professionals to police. Music that appeals to local youth is just one of the happy sounds emanating almost daily from this safe space.

With a budget of $240,000 — only one-third of which comes from the city — and weekday programs ranging from smoking cessation to political debate, THE GARAGE has about 500 registered young people participating in different education and recreation programs and an average of 600 unregistered drop-in youth per week; THE GARAGE also reaches thousands more through weekend music events. THE GARAGE recorded more than 30,000 visits by young people from Burnsville and the surrounding area to its programs and events in 2005.

"THE GARAGE keeps me out of trouble because the troublemakers don't want to go there... It's my favorite place. People actually 'get' kids and want to make an environment for them."

— One youth's response to THE GARAGE, a teen recreation center in Burnsville

Additional support and leadership for THE GARAGE comes from three overlapping sources:

- The City of Burnsville took the lead in redeveloping its facility for teen use, and now provides staff to administer programs, write proposals, build community partnerships, and maintain the facility. "The mayor's confidence is why the program works...not sure I could do this job without her support...it's a big risk," says Eric Billiet, manager of THE GARAGE.

- THE GARAGE Advisory Board develops and implements programs, outreach, and support services, and includes Mayor Elizabeth Kautz, a rotating group of three police officers, the Dakota County Public Health Department, and youth. "Once the police began to see that there was a real structure and philosophy at the center they started to respond more positively," Billiet explains. "The police have become liaisons...the chief has always been a supporter of the center and has made it clear to the Police Department: 'we will work with these youth.' Both the mayor and chief of police have embraced the argument that these successful collaborations can yield long-term reductions in crime."

- The third "leg of the stool" is the Burnsville Youth Center Foundation, which raises funds from local businesses and agencies such as civic organizations and Chamber of Commerce members.

Burnsville points to two major results from THE GARAGE and its philosophy of youth-led programming: delinquency prevention and reduction, and positive changes in the community's perception of teenagers. The "safe space" aspect of THE GARAGE creates an environment free from drugs and alcohol. Participating youth report decreases in substance abuse as well as unlawful behavior such as vandalism, theft, and fighting. Seventeen percent reported better school attendance, 25 percent reported getting along with teachers better, 21 percent reported more motivation to do well in school, and 33 percent reported an increase in good decision-making about drugs and alcohol. Nearly 40 percent of parents of participating youth report improvements in their children's behavior. "THE GARAGE has given my son a sense of being part of the community in which we live," reflects one Burnsville resident. The proportion of Burnsville residents reporting in 2003 that teens are listened to and valued was nearly twice as high as when THE GARAGE first opened its doors in 1999.

For other communities interested in pursuing a "safe space" approach, Burnsville recommends monitoring accomplishments and creating an air of accountability through participant and parent surveys and focus groups. "The mayor pays close attention to community surveys...they are what the city listens to," says Billiet. In addition, staff of THE GARAGE note that youth-led "participatory programming" requires greater staff effort. Last, staff members recommend consistent efforts to maintain relationships with all partners, as the success of THE GARAGE has depended upon the respect the center earns from the police, the mayor, and other community members.

Contact:

Eric J. Billiet, Manager
THE GARAGE
City of Burnsville
100 Civic Center Parkway
Burnsville, MN 55337
(952) 895-4578
eric.billiet@ci.burnsville.mn.us

Leadership Keys

Engaged youth in creating a safe and appealing environment.

Rather than setting up new programs for teens and hoping they would participate, the City of Burnsville ensured that programming at THE GARAGE was driven by teens. Because youth had a leading voice in deciding how the facility was used, THE GARAGE offered relevant and stimulating activities for area teens while at the same time providing them with a safe and supervised place to get together.

Measured results to bolster community support.

By using data to demonstrate how THE GARAGE promotes positive behavior among youth and changes adults' perceptions of teenagers, the city helped make the case to donors and community members for why the center should continue operating. The collection of these data to measure results also helped sustain the broad-based collaboration that is essential to the effectiveness of the model.

Creatively deployed city resources to focus on prevention.

By redeveloping a municipal garage and transforming it into a teen center, Burnsville found an innovative way to invest in its young people and seek long-term reductions in violence and risk-taking behaviors. City leaders are confident that this commitment to positive youth development will also yield savings over time, lowering future costs associated with juvenile crime and other antisocial activities.

El Paso, Texas

(pop. 598,590)

El Paso had threatened to put career criminologists out of business. During the 1990s, El Paso recorded one of the lowest crime rates in the nation for a city of its size, despite having a low average income, low educational attainment, and a high influx of immigrants — factors traditionally correlated with high crime rates.

In recent years, however, things began to change: gang activity increased and homicides spiked. The police department, with the full blessing of then-Mayor Larry Francis and city council, committed itself to stopping the violence and to "protecting and supporting our children and families." It began with a full re-examination of what it was doing and how.

The examination resulted in a prime strategic shift that has been sustained under the leadership of several mayors, including current Mayor John Cook: a redefinition of policing from "arrests to solving the problem." Officers increased their presence in schools, attended sports events, helped to staff summer camps, and coached teams. Police went into the community to learn more about residents' concerns. Relationships were forged not only with schools, but with recreation centers, health clinics, and the faith community. Relationships extended vertically into the community and horizontally across agencies in city government such as parks and recreation and zoning. The mayor, city manager, and city councilors were a constant presence, speaking at events, opening programs, presenting awards, creating inter- and intra-agency partnerships, and giving the police chief and his staff full rein for a strategy that, early on, showed signs of dramatic success.

Traditional programs such as Drug Abuse Resistance Education (DARE), the Police Athletic League, and school resource officers were revitalized, but the centerpiece became the creation and building of the Youth Initiative Program (YIP). YIP, a forum of 208 public and private member agencies from across the city, holds a police-chaired meeting on the third Thursday of each month. YIP brings together all facets of the community to provide "a networking forum that allows agencies and citizens to participate in addressing the problems that affect youth." YIP agencies work together to target and provide early identification and referral services for El Paso's at-risk youth and to develop youth programming.

YIP meetings are action-oriented work sessions focused on improving services and outcomes for youth through roundtable discussions of specific cases, prevention/intervention applications, and potential new programs. Service gaps and service duplication are identified. The core elements are built on the theoretical foundation of community oriented policing and cross-sector collaboration. They include the Multi-Agency Referral System (MARS), which provides the cooperative delivery of social services to students at a level where they can be further supported through their school, a Youth Helpline Directory of Services that is provided to the schools and community and updated continually on the police department web site, and a monthly newsletter that heralds community events, celebrates successes, flags problems, and provides tips on youth safety and development. YIP partners are dedicated to a holistic approach and through constant listening, critiquing, and total transparency, provide multilayered services, "from tattoo removal and truancy reduction to afterschool programs, teen health, and family support…doing whatever it takes…maybe all it takes is getting the family a refrigerator," says Lt. Alfred Lowe.

YIP has also been successful at filling service gaps by sharing accountability for specific cases. For example, one case presented at a MARS meeting involved a high school student not attending school because he was in a homeless shelter

"If the homicide rate continues to go down, I'm going to have to get a hobby."

— Lt. Alfred Lowe, Section Commander —
Crimes Against Persons, El Paso Police Department

and had no transportation. He was further disadvantaged by having only one arm. Through agency-school collaboration, he was provided transportation, basic needs, and guidance. These services helped him graduate from high school. He later received two scholarships to the University of Texas at El Paso, worked there as a security guard, and moved into his own apartment. Further, a local doctor provided him with a prosthetic arm. The student now plays the guitar and wrote and sang a song in thanks to the community.

Another case involving a student referred to MARS because of truancy and declining grades revealed that his family duty was to take care of an elderly grandparent. Services were secured for the grandparent so that the student could attend school. He also received tutoring and counseling.

El Paso combines both process and outcome measures. Process measures include the number of agencies attending the monthly meetings, the growing number of youth enrolled in programs, and the number of families served. In terms of outcomes, there has been a steady decline in youth arrested since 1999, including a 20 percent drop from 2003 to 2004. In addition, the total number of homicides was 14 in 2005, and as of late November 2006, there have been 13 homicides.

The city is clear about the core elements needed for replication. The primary element is attitude, a belief that "we're in it together, helping kids, making El Paso the safest city in the country," and that a city must commit itself to a community-wide campaign based on the realization that the city simply will not work unless in full partnership with its citizens. The embracing vision must include stopping crime and serving children and

The primary element is attitude, a belief that "we're in it together, helping kids, making El Paso the safest city in the country."

families: "It will die if you just focus on crime. That's important, but we have to look at having good things happen for kids." Implicit is the belief that enforcement, prevention, and intervention are part of a natural whole. Information sharing is vital, along with looking at others as partners instead of competitors. "We needed a central clearinghouse, and we needed everybody's buy in." Services had to be "across the board."

Then there is a dimension not often recognized or practiced, namely, a predisposition to change: "We're flexible. Needs change. For instance, out of 14 homicides last year, six were because of domestic violence. So this year, we're starting a domestic violence program. I told my guys, 'You're on this job now, but it will probably be only for two years. Don't get too comfortable. Things change.'" Crime changes. Communities change. If a program becomes fixed, it will eventually either wither or become irrelevant and unresponsive to new community needs.

"Finally," advises Lowe, "when you bring your people together monthly, make sure to feed them."

Contact:

Nell Tovar, Coordinator
Youth Initiative Program
El Paso Police Department
9600 Dyer Street
El Paso, TX 79924
(915) 298-9604
TovarM@ci.el-paso.tx.us

~

Leadership Keys

● **Embraced a broad vision of child and family well-being.**

City leaders and police reframed El Paso's approach to public
safety by focusing greater attention on underlying problems
facing local residents. This shift is reflected in how the community
now measures its progress: while continuing to track key indicators such as youth homicides and arrest rates, El Paso also gauges
whether it is reaching youth and families with critical programs
and services designed to address their needs.

● **Dramatically expanded community oriented policing and
collaboration.**

As police became immersed in all facets of community life, new
partnership opportunities emerged. Both police and top city
leaders worked across internal boundaries and engaged other key
institutions in the community. The Youth Initiative Program
institutionalizes and sustains this commitment to collaboration
on behalf of the city's youth.

● **Remained flexible, responding to changing circumstances
and needs.**

The widespread collaboration between city leaders, law enforcement officials, and community partners has enhanced the city's
ability to respond to emerging trends and new developments.
This constant re-examination of priorities and openness to
change increases the likelihood that El Paso will identify and
address new challenges quickly and effectively.

New Brighton, Minnesota

(pop. 20,738)

In 1995, the City of New Brighton Public Safety Police Division (NBPS) noted a significant increase in calls for service from a 364-unit apartment complex in the heart of the city known as Polynesian Village. New Brighton, once a quiet suburb, found itself confronted with crimes more typically experienced in urban areas. "Crime shot up," said then-City Manager Matt Fulton. "Neighbors complained; halls were in chaos; parties went on all the time, and the crime became like inner-city crimes — open air drug dealing, assaults, prostitution." Even worse, certain residents were becoming increasingly hostile toward the city. "Firemen couldn't even respond to alarms sometimes because of people loitering in the halls. When responding to one arson call, the police were surrounded by hostile neighbors. It was very, very volatile," observes Bob Jacobson, New Brighton's director of public safety.

Crime — and the dramatic increase in the number and severity of calls for services — spurred the city to act. But concern for children and youth was an equally important spur. "Kids were not supervised," says Jacobson. "We didn't want our kids to get hurt, victimized, or improperly influenced. We wanted our kids cared for, fed well, and away from the bad influences — away from fights, drug dealing, and negative adults."

"We didn't want our kids to get hurt, victimized, or improperly influenced. We wanted our kids cared for, fed well, and away from the bad influences — away from fights, drug dealing, and negative adults."

— Bob Jacobson, director of public safety, City of New Brighton

Working in concert, the city council, NBPS, and Mayor Steve Larson created a four-part strategy. Its most dramatic innovation was the passage of a landmark ordinance aimed at apartment complex owners. If calls for service exceeded a certain number, licensing costs went up to cover the service. If calls kept coming in, the license itself was put in jeopardy. Said Fulton, "We hit them in the pocket book." Half-funded by licensing fines, the city created a "Crime-Free Multi-Housing Officer" position and set up a Multi-Housing Managers Coalition to provide a forum for airing issues, affixing responsibility, and solving problems.

The second part of the strategy involved enhanced neighborhood-oriented policing. Police increased their visibility. A satellite office staffed by a neighborhood officer was set up in the complex. Residents were invited to drop in. The department offered free fingerprinting, "KID Care" pamphlets to assist in identifying children in the event of a lost child or abduction, and fire and police station tours. Crime watch groups were formed. City councilors, the mayor, and the police chief attended neighborhood get-togethers. Police officers offered a "Krispy Kreme with a Kop" time to encourage residents to share concerns. Citizens were encouraged to attend the nine-week Citizens Police Academy and seven-week Emergency Response Team training. The annual "National Night Out" was recognized as one of the most successful (and largest) in the nation.

The third strategy focused on NBPS responding swiftly and thoroughly to all incidents. The citizens felt unprotected, as if NBPS did not have things in control. NBPS discovered that its response rate to citizen complaints could be improved to visibly reassure the public, and as a strategy to directly discourage criminal activity in targeted neighborhoods.

The creation of the "Poly Partners" coalition is the fourth component of the strategy and demonstrates the city's commitment to community empowerment, service provision, and improvement in the quality of life. Partners included city agencies such as NBPS and the parks and recreation department, schools, community groups such as Youth and Family Services, the faith sector, business leaders, and the newly-formed Community Partnership for Youth on whose board the city manager sits. Tutoring, mentoring, recreation, and afterschool initiatives are among the programs offered. Poly Partnership goals include decreasing resident turnover, decreasing the crime rate, providing residents with opportunities for personal growth, and instilling within residents a sense of ownership.

The city is proud of the results this partnership has achieved. An evaluation conducted by the Amherst H. Wilder Foundation in 2003 found that:

- 96 percent of respondents were either satisfied or very satisfied with police responses to calls, a jump from 90 percent in 2001.

- 91 percent were either satisfied or very satisfied with how they were treated by the police, compared with 75 percent in 2001.

- More than 50 percent of residents reported less or much less graffiti and gang activity.

- The number of people stating that they felt safe rose from 55 percent in 2001 to 77 percent in 2003.

- Calls to the police dropped by a stunning 50 percent, from 1,200 in 2001 to 600 in 2003.

"I have to say, when you have success, momentum develops. Everybody is excited and is confirmed in this new way of doing business."

— Matt Fulton, former city manager, City of New Brighton

Fulton says the New Brighton model is "absolutely replicable." The core elements include: full commitment by city leaders, both administratively and in terms of visibility; a commitment to community oriented policing; partnering with the community to provide services and to reaffirm expectations and responsibilities; clarity of expectations (and obligations) to apartment complex owners; and a commitment to measuring results, which are fed back to city and community partners.

"I have to say," concludes Fulton, "when you have success, momentum develops. Everybody is excited and is confirmed in this new way of doing business."

In 2004, the City of New Brighton won the International Association of Chiefs of Police Community Policing Award, and in 2005 the National League of Cities honored the city with the silver award in the James C. Howland Awards for Municipal Enrichment for this community policing partnership.

Contact:

Mayor Steve Larson
City of New Brighton
803 Old Highway 8, NW
New Brighton, MN 55112
(651) 636-4997
stevenlarson1@comcast.net

Leadership Keys

● **Used municipal policies to create new incentives for violence prevention.**

By increasing licensing costs for the owners of apartment complexes that were the source of high numbers of calls to the police department, the city promoted shared responsibility for the safety of the apartments. This system of graduated licensing fees also contributed to the city's overall community policing strategy by opening up a funding stream to support new problem-solving efforts.

● **Improved community relations through enhanced neighborhood policing.**

The Amherst H. Wilder Foundation's evaluation results highlight a remarkable turnaround in the relationship between apartment complex residents and police. By establishing a more visible presence at the apartments, increasing outreach, and opening new lines of communication with local residents, city leaders and police officers have increased levels of trust throughout the community.

● **Formed partnerships to empower residents.**

The partnerships between city leaders, the police, schools, businesses, and community groups have allowed the city to focus on issues of neighborhood and family stability, as well as opportunities for youth development. Particularly in a small community such as New Brighton, city officials would otherwise find it very difficult to tackle these challenges on their own.

New Haven, Connecticut

(pop. 124,791)

In the early 1990s, America seemed to be awash in violence — the first Iraq war, gang wars and killings, and, close to home, the grisly murder of a young mother in New Haven. New Haven's former Chief of Police Nick Pastore, at the home of the murder victim while forensic evidence was being collected, suddenly came upon young children frozen in fear, sitting on a couch. When the chief thought about how little the police had to offer these children and the likelihood that officers would encounter them again, either as victims or perpetrators of future crime, he reached out to former Yale Child Study Center Director Dr. Donald Cohen, and the two leaders began what would become a model partnership.

The Child Development-Community Policing Program (CDCP), created soon thereafter, was concerned that trauma experienced by children could later explode if not handled properly. "We needed help. We knew we needed to understand the issue," says Captain Stephen Verrelli of the Department of Police Services. "The time issue is critical. Cops see the issue now. The clinicians see the results years later. We cannot let so much time pass. Early victims of crime often become perpetrators." The initiative establishes a part-

31

nership between the city and local university to explore community-focused strategies. The initiative's mission, "to heal the wounds that chronic exposure to violence inflicts on children," embraces extensive activity and detailed operating procedures developed since the program began in 1991.

Dr. Steven Marans, director of the National Center for Children Exposed to Violence, helped create the partnership. One cornerstone of the police-mental health relationship is developing an understanding of each other's work. "We train them in child development," says Marans, "and clinicians learn about policing. Rookie cops get eight hours of training in child development and trauma response at the police academy, veteran officers get regular in-service training, and supervisors get advanced seminars. Senior officers teach a seminar for clinicians in police procedures and we continue to learn from observing on ride-alongs." Marans makes the unusual observation that good police and clinical work are linked: "A sense of safety and security is needed before adequate clinical work can begin. Sometimes external order is needed to set the context for healing." Current Police Chief Francisco Ortiz agrees that policing and support for families go together. "Addressing the needs of children and families in our community is what police officers do every day of the week. It's the most important part of our work."

Marans' assertion is played out operationally. Police, clinicians, child protective service, and juvenile justice staffers meet weekly to discuss cases. Following a shooting or a particularly violent event, police go through the neighborhood knocking on doors explaining what happened and leaving pamphlets about changes parents can expect from their children following their exposure to violence and how to contact their local police officer or the Child Study Center. "This gives two messages," says Verrelli, "that what happened is not right, and that we care."

Marans claims that support by Mayor John DeStefano, Jr., is essential. "He has opened the city to us, helping us get into the schools, letting us train all his departments, bringing in Homeland Security…and, of greatest importance, he and the city council support us during budget time. It's not just MOUs. The mayor's people are *fully* involved, case conferences, staff donated in kind, all of that."

The partnership among the city, police, Yale Child Study Center, probation, child protection, and other community agencies rests firmly on a commitment to community oriented policing and extensive communication. Police are deployed throughout the city, and neighborhood-based substations support both police and community activity. Verrelli asserts that "Community oriented policing means we keep our guys in the neighborhood. Some of the guys are in neighborhoods on bikes. Their job is to know the players. We do prevention and intervention. For example, we show up unannounced at the door of a person convicted of domestic violence. The accused knows he's being watched, the victim knows we are available, the kids know we care, and everybody feels safer."

The CDCP program is one of the prime reasons that crime in New Haven has dropped by 61 percent since 1991. Victims of domestic violence feel more comfortable with the police and call for less serious incidents rather than waiting until there is a dire emergency. School resource officers, present in all New Haven schools, provide surveillance, get to know the kids, and help them get into after-school programs. Demands for the Child Study Center's services have increased. Crime reporting has gone up, meaning that citizens increasingly trust the police.

The most striking sign of success is that the program is no longer a program. It has been institutionalized. "It's another tool on our belts," says Verrelli. "Working together has become a way of doing business," says Marans. "It informs everything we do, from training to emergency response to delivery of clinical services. Both officers and mental health professionals in New Haven have developed a new way of thinking about children and families caught up in violence, and that isn't going to go away."

Contacts:

Capt. Stephen Verrelli
New Haven Department of Police Services
One Union Avenue
New Haven, CT 06519
(203) 946-6966

Dr. Steven Marans, Director
National Center for Children Exposed to Violence
230 South Frontage Road
New Haven, CT 06520-7900
(203) 785-7047
nccev@info.med.yale.edu

Leadership Keys

● **Built upon leadership commitments rooted in personal experience.**

The police chief witnessed the traumatic impact that violence has on children throughout the community and provided strong support for New Haven's innovative response. Similarly, the mayor and his key staff were directly involved in the development and operations of the Child Development-Community Policing Program. This first-hand engagement by city and police leaders has sustained the initiative through multiple budget cycles and enabled New Haven to bring together different systems in pursuit of a common goal.

● **Leveraged local university support.**

The articulation of a focused goal by city leaders — "healing the wounds that chronic exposure to violence inflicts on children" — provided an opportunity for the city to tap valuable university resources and expertise. The resulting partnership between the New Haven police department and the Yale Child Study Center created a context for learning that has helped each partner improve its effectiveness and led to a new focus on prevention and intervention that did not previously exist.

● **Took multiple steps to build trust between residents and police.**

Police have offered families additional support and increased their presence in schools and neighborhoods. In the process, community relations have improved and residents are more likely to turn to police officers for help.

Sallisaw, Oklahoma

(pop. 8,621)

Sallisaw, Oklahoma, is one of many places in rural America that have felt the effects of violence and lawlessness among methamphetamine users and dealers. Particularly worrisome to town leaders has been the exposure of children to drugs, domestic violence, and other negative influences. As a supplement to ongoing law enforcement efforts, city leaders determined to fight back directly on behalf of, and with, Sallisaw's children. This determination took shape as Student Heroes in Everyday Living Decisions (SHIELD), a drug abuse awareness and education program in which police officers begin teaching anti-drug messages, anti-bullying, and anger management skills as early as kindergarten.

One way to view SHIELD is as a "bridge" between the office of Mayor Shannon Vann, the police department, the schools, and other city agencies such as the Parks and Recreation Department. SHIELD also draws support from the city manager, civic organizations such as the Lions and Rotary Clubs, and churches. SHIELD grew out of programs operated under federal Drug Abuse Resistance Education (DARE) and Office of Community Oriented Policing Services (COPS) grants.

As a supplement to ongoing law enforcement
efforts, city leaders determined to fight back
directly on behalf of, and with,
Sallisaw's children.

The Police Department stations a school resource officer (SRO) on the elementary school campus full-time during the school year. The SRO helps raise students' awareness of the danger of drug abuse by discussing "bad things to put in your body," and has expanded age-appropriate education and drug awareness programs for all elementary school grades. The SRO also serves as an instructor and developer of police reserve schools, which allow for certification of reserve officers who back up the full-time police force for patrols and big events after extensive training (many become full-time officers in the future). In addition, the police chief started a student police academy that helps students learn about basic police work and receive a certificate of completion. A formal agreement between the school superintendent and city manager underlies this arrangement. The five-week SHIELD program involves classes that take place one hour per week for students in fifth grade, and follow an instructor's manual and workbooks.

As top city leaders, the mayor and police chief play active roles in the oversight of SHIELD. The town's police chief and school resource officer keep the mayor involved by detailing success stories and jointly brainstorming ways to constantly improve the program. The chief of police has made specialized training for the SRO available via the annual municipal budget, and has assigned a colorful special vehicle to the SRO as well.

The mayor and chief of police participate together in SHIELD course "graduations" and honors each year, along with the fire chief, city councilmembers, and school board members. The mayor's role in SHIELD also extends to "setting the climate for what will be done in schools." For instance, the mayor and the city council established a "no tolerance" policy regarding violence in school. In addition, the assistant chief of police and city manager provided full support to a senior police officer to develop the program.

The police department's reporting systems suggest that SHIELD's lessons have helped in reducing violence and substance abuse. The city's success with the five-week SHIELD course for fifth graders has prompted development of an educational program for younger students as well. The governor of Oklahoma has recognized the success of the program with additional funding in the form of a Governor's Safe Schools grant. In addition, teachers, principals, and officers on the street testify that greater awareness of drug-related dangers has lessened incidents of drug abuse.

City officials in Sallisaw point to continuity in personnel as having played a key role in the development and sustainability of the program. Sharing the cost of the SRO salary between Sallisaw schools and the police department during the school year has also added longevity to the program. Sallisaw estimates that a community of similar size could launch a program such as SHIELD at a cost (excluding salary) of some $8,000 for program supplies, travel, and training, with ongoing costs thereafter of $5,000 per year.

Contact:

Chief Shaloa Edwards
Sallisaw Police Department
101 West Chickasaw
Sallisaw, OK 74955
(918) 775-4177
901pd@diamondnet.us

Leadership Keys

- **Intervened at early ages to combat drug abuse.**

  The SHIELD program responded to the growth of methamphetamine use among young people by seeking to educate children in elementary schools about the dangers of drug abuse. Support from the mayor and police chief has underscored the value that Sallisaw places on early prevention efforts and leverages state resources to carry out the program.

- **Launched a partnership with the school system to ensure sustainability.**

  Leadership from the mayor and police chief also created a climate of collaboration throughout the community, underscoring that both the city and the schools have a compelling interest in preventing drug abuse and keeping young people safe. The partnership with the school district resulted in a commitment to joint funding of a school resource officer, a structure that greatly enhances the sustainability of the SHIELD program.

- **Provided staff training and benefits to promote continuity.**

  Specialized training and designation of a distinctive police vehicle for use by the school resource officer represented two ways in which the chief of police signaled his support for the SHIELD program. By avoiding turnover in this critical staff position, Sallisaw has been able to keep the initiative growing and on track.

San José, California

(pop. 912,332)

The broad-based Mayor's Gang Prevention Task Force in San José, and the $3 million annual Bringing Everyone's Strengths Together (BEST) funding mechanism that the task force oversees, are structures that have evolved over the past 15 years to meet changing needs while helping San José maintain its status as the nation's safest large city. Efforts led by the Task Force have helped reduce the per capita rate of violent crime in the city by 53 percent between 1994 and 2003 and lower Juvenile Hall admits by 59 percent between 1994 to 2004. Also of note, the task force tag line has changed from the original "Project Neighborhood Crackdown" to today's "Reclaiming Our Youth."

San José started down this path when persistent faith-based community organizers began asking then-Mayor Susan Hammer to coordinate a response to the 300 percent rise in the violent juvenile crime rate that occurred in the late 1980s. The pleas of one outspoken mother for the city to help see her daughter safely through to adulthood resonated with the mayor and her agency heads and prompted action. Former Mayor Ron Gonzales continued this effort in recent years, working closely with city managers, police chiefs, and the community to reduce violence and make sure young people feel and stay connected.

The now time-tested structure in San José has the Task Force carrying its work forward through frequent meetings of a Technical Team of "worker bees" drawn from city and county agencies and community-based organizations, as well as a regular convening of a Policy Team of leaders (including the mayor, police chief, business, probation). Community-based organizations such as faith-based People Acting in Community Together (PACT) and gang intervention experts from California Youth Outreach, along with the state parole office and U.S. Attorney, also participate.

Each year, depending on conditions in the city, the Task Force determines a new ratio for guiding the distribution of available funds among BEST grantees — 30 grants of $5,000 to $225,000 — depending on the assessed need for prevention or intervention services. BEST grants operate within an asset-building framework, and grantees are subject to rigorous performance monitoring. Each grantee organization must also establish its qualifications by responding to a Request for Qualifications (RFQ), and must provide matching funds.

Every three years, the Task Force goes through a formal process of rethinking its strategy and objectives based on an assessment of changing community realities. The process includes an annual retreat of the Policy and Technical Teams, community input solicited through a BEST needs assessment, and a close review of the results of annual BEST evaluations. The current strategic plan emphasizes a new intervention-based strategy with several key elements. An example of the evaluation efforts that occurs through this planning process is the determination to spend 70% of BEST funds on intervention — as opposed to 39 percent and 54 percent, respectively, in the last two grant cycles.

Police Department cooperation and involvement with community-based BEST grantees is substantial. Crime prevention specialists teach children how to use thinking skills to avoid trouble, intervention teams handle escalating threats, and a Police Activities League provides social activities. In addition to these roles, the Police Department also leads the city's gang-prevention efforts.

Overall leadership for San José's efforts begins with the mayor, who calls and chairs the monthly Task Force meetings and relies on staff from two city departments for briefings and support (the Department of Parks, Recreation, and Neighborhood Services and the Police Department). The mayor's leadership role also comes through at budget time, when he can use his final budget authority to ensure funding for BEST. Indeed, mayoral leadership has proven critical in a city with a trim police force, widely varying socioeconomic conditions in different parts of the city, 19 school districts, and a county government that fulfills many social services functions. Sitting alongside the mayor at Task Force meetings are the chief of police and key police lieutenants, as well as school superintendents or their deputies. Nationally prominent retired Superior Court Judge Leonard P. Edwards also has provided leadership through his consistent emphasis on multi-sided collaboration from his longstanding post presiding over Santa Clara County Juvenile Dependency Court, which serves San José.

A recent third-party evaluation of accomplishments shows the beneficial effects of just one year of BEST funding. Connections with caring adults grew, as BEST program staff "indicated that their customers developed caring relationships with an average of 3.9 new adults due to their BEST services." On the "customer satisfaction" front, child and youth customers gave BEST services an overall positive customer satisfaction rating of 85 percent in 2004-05 and 83 percent in 2005-06, while parents have given satisfaction ratings as high as 89 percent.

San José notes that the Task Force approach could be adopted by "any community in which the participants are committed to common goals, communication, coordination, and cooperation." Further, San José recommends "keeping youth safety as the overarching goal" in order to work through differences.

Contact:

Esther G. Mota, Community Services Supervisor
City of San José
Parks, Recreation & Neighborhood Services
645 Wool Creek Drive, Suite 97
San José, CA   95112
(408) 277-2741
esther.mota@sanjoseca.gov

Leadership Keys

● **Used a two-tier structure to set policy and follow through on implementation.**

The creation of both a Policy Team composed of top municipal, law enforcement, and community leaders and a Technical Team charged with translating vision into concrete actions has given the Gang Prevention Task Force great strength and versatility. This structure enables San José to address important implementation challenges without losing sight of larger policy goals and objectives.

● **Adjusted funding priorities in response to changing needs.**

The Task Force's periodic review process and community needs assessment has helped the city adapt to new challenges (e.g., the perceived need for a greater focus on intervention). The thorough monitoring of BEST grantees' performance also maximizes the city's investment in Task Force efforts.

● **Provided consistent, high-profile leadership.**

Active participation by the mayor, police chief, school superintendents, prominent judges, the city manager, and other top leaders have made Task Force initiatives a high priority. City, county, and community partners are all held accountable for helping San José retain its reputation for being a safe city.

More City Examples

This section highlights ten additional cities in which a specific problem motivated municipal and law enforcement officials to establish new partnerships that promote the safety and well-being of children and youth.

Chula Vista, California (pop. 210,497) — Bullying Prevention

Out of a strong desire to "put prevention first," the Police Department in suburban Chula Vista has worked with the elementary school district and city family resource centers as a lead U.S. implementer of the Olweus Bullying Prevention Program. The Olweus program, which was launched in Chula Vista in 2003, caught the city's eye because studies in Norway, where it took shape, showed that it reduced bullying behavior by 50 percent through a combination of community involvement and clear rules. The city's interest in bullying also stems from noticing just how often violence, truancy, and adult crimes involve those with a history or current involvement in bullying — and that the impact on victims of bullying can be severe.

Implementation of the Olweus approach began with surveys of students, teachers, and parents in English and Spanish at three pilot elementary schools. Police Department school resource officers then joined teachers, principals, and parents on bullying prevention committees for each school, received training from a national expert, prepared implementation plans, and conducted parent meetings. The plans emphasized "reducing the opportunity for students to bully," behavioral expectations, and consequences. Early results analyzed through the Police Department's in-house data collection capacity have been promising in pilot school sites. Fewer students reported being chronically bullied or participating in bullying. Parents saw the school-city-police collaborative handling bullying with greater seriousness. The promising results have prompted additional district schools to adopt the bullying prevention program.

Contact:

Melanie Culuko, Public Safety Analyst
Chula Vista Police Department
315 Fourth Avenue
Chula Vista, CA 91910
(619) 476-2310
mculuko@chulavistapd.org

Fort Worth, Texas (pop. 624,067) — Safe City Commission

In pursuit of a lofty objective — becoming the safest major city in the U.S. — Fort Worth's mayor and a host of city, county, state, and federal public safety officials, along with business and community leaders, came together to form Safe City Commission, Inc. This nonprofit organization, in addition to its role in fostering collaboration among public safety and crime prevention agencies, helps train and support community champions for crime prevention, safety, education, and law enforcement. In one example of its particular focus on the safety of children, the Commission coordinates a 200-member collaborative anti-gang network known as Community Organizations for Restoration and Empowerment (CORE).

The Commission's response to youth violence has also taken the form of an "Imagine No Violence" citywide art contest sponsored in partnership with the local school districts — an idea that sprang from high school students themselves. Building on the success of the art contest, in which more than 20,000 students participate each year, the Commission, Fort Worth Police Department, and Texas Wesleyan University recently launched a new gang and youth violence prevention initiative for sixth, seventh, and eighth graders. This effort, dubbed Bright Futures, prevents gang involvement among youth at greatest risk of future gang membership through instruction and activities with gang unit police officers. Bright Futures also provides a thorough course in life skills, as well as academic support.

Contact:

Ken Shetter, Executive Director
Safe City Commission
200 Calhoun Street
Fort Worth, TX 76102
(817) 885-7774
kshetter@safecitycommission.org

Los Angeles, California (pop. 3,844,829) — Gang Reduction Program

Continuing high gang participation and violence, as well as a high incarceration rate for young gang members, prompted the Los Angeles mayor, police, and two city departments to blend prevention, intervention, and enforcement into a strategy that previously included only strong doses of enforcement. Out of this commitment, and with one of four special federal grants to reduce gang violence as well as matching city funds directed by the mayor, the Gang Reduction Program (GRP) took shape.

Key GRP partners include the police department, city attorney's office, school district, district attorney, other enforcement agencies, juvenile probation, Homeboy Industries, community- and faith-based organizations, and the Department of Homeland Security and Public Safety (for administration). The three objectives of the initiative are to help keep kids out of gangs, stem deeper involvement among those already in gangs, and help keep gang members who are returning from juvenile corrections from rejoining gangs. Notably, work begins with community assessment at the neighborhood level — what's working, what's not, and what citizens want based on focus groups.

Examples of GRP efforts include prenatal and infancy support for first-time mothers living in gang-involved environments, mentoring for young males without positive male role models within the home, afterschool and recreational programs, early college awareness and literacy programs for fourth- and fifth-grade students and their parents, case management for middle school youth, and gang awareness training for community members, schools, and parents.

Youth ages 14 to 22 who are actively involved in a gang and want to leave the gang receive the opportunity to enroll in vocational education, community college, or high school completion programs, and have access to services such as tattoo removal, legal assistance, job training and placement, substance abuse/alcohol treatment, and anger management classes. An example of an approach other cities could borrow from GRP is the "Referral Ticket." This form, filled out in triplicate by police officers, juvenile probation officers, and school personnel, goes to the young person, his or her parents, and GRP. GRP is then able to follow up and offer services.

Contact:

Mildred Martinez, Coordinator
Gang Reduction Program
Mayor's Office of Homeland Security and Public Safety
200 North Spring Street, Room 303
Los Angeles, CA 90012
(213) 978-0686
Mildred.Martinez@LAcity.org

Los Gatos, California (pop. 28,029) — Youth Party Guidelines

As an outgrowth of a community conversation spurred by the death of a teenager leaving a party where alcohol was served, the Los Gatos/Monte Sereno Police Department instituted a new way of responding to party complaints. The suburban city's 2005 Youth Party Guidelines constitute what might be called a mutual obligation pact between police, parents, and young people. Under the guidelines, police react to reports of loud or unlawful parties in a measured way — with a phone call first and an officer's visit later. In turn, parents or others are expected to notify police in advance of concerns about possible unlawful activities at youth parties.

Los Gatos' approach rests on a backbone of community policing and on active participation by the schools, businesses, community groups, and city leaders in addition to parents and students. The city established a "Party Notification Line" phone number which any parent, young person, or other community member may call in advance. If a complaint comes in, the police dispatcher contacts the person responsible for the party. Notably, the guidelines also call for the police to coordinate actively with numerous other stakeholders, including schools, neighboring communities' police and sheriff departments, and the state alcoholic beverage control department.

Contact:

Sergeant Randy Rimple
Los Gatos/Monte Sereno Police Department
110 East Main Street
Los Gatos, CA 95031
(408) 354-6843
rrimple@losgatosca.gov

Mount Vernon, New York (pop. 67,924) — Gang Resistance Education And Training

In response to a series of violent events that occurred during a brief period, the City of Mount Vernon wanted to take action with a collaborative and systematic approach. Leadership came from the mayor, working with the Mount Vernon Community That Cares Coalition, which consists of representatives of the city, police department, schools, youth bureau, social service agencies, parents, and youth. The city and coalition decided to implement an anti-gang, anti-violence initiative to reduce risk factors, using funding available through a federal Drug-Free Communities grant.

The coalition chose to implement the widely used Gang Resistance Education And Training (G.R.E.A.T.) curriculum, which was developed through a combined effort of the United States Bureau of Alcohol, Tobacco, Firearms and Explosives and the Phoenix Police Department in 1991. Police officers are the instructors for this school-based curriculum, the primary objective of which is prevention. Curriculum components are available for use in four settings: middle and elementary schools, summer programs, and family training sessions. One of the ways G.R.E.A.T. responds to Mount Vernon's original concern is that it emphasizes using means other than violence to solve problems. The reach of the program continues to expand through creative strategies such as a "Youth Day" in which children who participate in the G.R.E.A.T. program share the positive aspects of the program with peers and parents who have not yet been exposed to the curriculum.

Contact:

Daniella Jackson, Research & Grants Administrator
City of Mount Vernon
One Roosevelt Square
Mount Vernon, NY 10550
914-699-7230 x132
djackson@cmvny.com

Philadelphia, Pennsylvania (pop. 1,463,281) — Youth Violence Reduction Partnership

Philadelphia's response to continuing high youth violence in certain parts of the city was to initiate the Youth Violence Reduction Partnership (YVRP). YVRP focuses on young people ages 12 to 24 who are most at risk of killing or being killed. These youth receive a combination of intensive surveillance and supportive services in an effort to deter their involvement in violent activities.

Leadership for YVRP comes from the District Attorney's Office (which chairs the Steering Committee) and the city's Cabinet-level Managing Director's Office (which coordinates the ongoing activities of the partner agencies). Active participants include a broad group of agencies: the police, adult and juvenile probation departments, a private agency that provides "streetworkers" who assist in providing positive supports to the youth in the program, family court, the local human services department (which provides support services to both the youth and their families), the school district, the housing authority, and a second private agency that provides data collection, program monitoring, and evaluation. Such broad collaboration has enabled YVRP to knit together comprehensive, coordinated services which young people experience as a combination of home visits, case management, and assistance in finding jobs and educational opportunities.

How does YVRP work? Youth identified through past involvement in, or proximity to, violence become "youth partners" of YVRP. Youth partners receive frequent home visits from probation officers, police, and streetworkers. Positive supports (such as help getting jobs) are provided by the streetworkers from a private, community-based agency. The probation officer acts as the case manager as teams of streetworkers, probation officers, and police work together to provide supports and improve surveillance and intelligence.

YVRP is currently in five of the city's 25 police districts and is planning to expand as funds become available. Researchers have tracked progress from the earliest days, and have shown that continued progress has been made in reducing the rate of homicides in the districts in which YVRP operates, compared to other non-YVRP police districts and the city as a whole.

Contact:

Denise Clayton, Coordinator
Youth Violence Reduction Partnership
1401 John F. Kennedy Boulevard, Room 10-003
Philadelphia, PA 19102
(215) 686-4595
denise.clayton@phila.gov

Providence, Rhode Island (pop. 176,862) — Providence Reentry Steering Committee

Given the disproportionate impact of crime on certain neighborhoods, and the number of incarcerated individuals from those neighborhoods, Providence's mayor and police chief designed a prisoner reentry program in early 2006. The initiative as currently envisioned will include youth returning from juvenile facilities.

Program success depends on wraparound services, cooperation among city and community entities, and a shift in how police see and carry out their work. The Providence Reentry Steering Committee — made up of representatives from the mayor's office, mental health, social services, substance abuse, housing, community and faith-based entities, and the police — recommends policy, monitors the work, and assesses results. Each of the nine police districts has established a mini-steering committee that mirrors the citywide committee.

The Providence initiative is one of several interrelated and coordinated efforts to address reentry issues across the state. There is interest in the Governor's Office, the State Department of Corrections, and among General Assembly leadership to address prisoner reentry. For example, in 2006, advocates were successful in getting voter approval for a state constitutional amendment that restores the right to vote for ex-offenders.

Contact:

Garry Bliss, Director of Policy
City of Providence
25 Dorrance Street
Providence, RI 02903
(401) 421-7740
gbliss@providenceri.com

Sheboygan, Wisconsin (pop. 48,872) — Neighbors Against Drugs

Faced with a crack cocaine epidemic that hit later than in many other places, Sheboygan adopted a civil response strategy known as Neighbors Against Drugs (NAD) to empower residents to stop drug dealing in their immediate neighborhood. In this strategy, a police officer trains residents and landlords to spot and bring community pressure against drug dealers, and also stands ready to use civil procedures to hold property owners responsible for failing to abate the nuisance. Residents post "Neighbors Against Drugs" signs at all but the suspected house on a block. The police and residents use the media to create a stir. Residents hold victory parties after dealers are evicted, move out, or otherwise stop dealing.

Neighbors Against Drugs grew out of a five-month planning effort involving community volunteers, city and business leaders, and a community police officer. The first 27 months of NAD resulted in "victories" in 22 neighborhoods, and the elimination of 62 drug houses. In one neighborhood, which had 11 suspected drug houses within four city blocks, Neighbors Against Drugs has helped reduce calls for police service by 36 percent, burglaries by 93 percent, theft by 92 percent, and vehicle theft by 100 percent. Through the process, neighborhood building occurs where connections may previously have been weak.

Detailed surveys show higher levels of civic interaction, which have contributed to healthier neighborhoods and lower crime. Residents surveyed also expressed a greater perception of safety and willingness to call the police or talk to their neighbors. Based on this model, Sheboygan has implemented three additional, similar programs — Students Against Drugs, Employers Against Drugs, and Bars Against Drugs — that focus on creating a healthier community and getting help to those who need it.

Contact:

Officer Todd Priebe
Sheboygan Police Department
828 Center Avenue
Sheboygan, WI 53081-4499
(920) 459-3341
tpriebe@ci.sheboygan.wi.us

Tupelo, Mississippi (pop. 35,673) — Police Athletic League

Faced with a rising incidence of gang violence and delinquency, the Tupelo Police Department worked with other city leaders and agencies to develop its first Police Athletic League (PAL) facility — thus joining the ranks of many other cities and towns using PALs as a crime prevention and youth development strategy. The city and department, with the support of the county judge, applied to the state for start-up funds. The mayor, city council president, and soon the entire council signed on as early backers of the initiative. One councilwoman now even runs a summer art camp for participants. Earlier, this high level of support paved the way for the city to administer the start-up grant and endorse a lease for space to be converted and equipped as a PAL center.

The new center relies mostly on male police officers, who serve as mentors and positive role models for at-risk young men whose fathers are absent from the home. Programs offer organized sports, recreation, and education, ranging from boxing to computer skills training. Notably, Tupelo's Youth Court will provide referrals to PAL — a type of alternative disposition of cases eagerly sought by the court. Private-sector partners include 25 businesspeople serving on an advisory board with an eye toward sustaining the program, and property managers of the city's most troubled rental property areas.

Contact:

Sergeant Michael Russell, Executive Director
Tupelo Police Athletic League
419 Robert E. Lee Drive
Tupelo, MS 38801
(662) 840-2535
michaelarussell@gmail.com

Worcester, Massachusetts (pop. 175,898) — Youth Mentoring Program

Worcester illustrates what a mid-sized city can do to adapt youth violence reduction approaches from larger cities. Specifically, the mayor and police chief brainstormed and then led a drive to bring the most relevant aspects of Boston's Ten Point Coalition, a group of local clergy that united to work with the city and police department to combat youth violence, to their city. The result was the Youth Mentoring Program (YMP). Key community partners to which the mayor and police chief reached out included the local black clergy and an interfaith group. A top priority was to establish a sense of trust and communication between the clergy and law enforcement officials. With that sense of trust in place, the program could develop as a way of connecting young people with caring adults drawn from faith-based organizations.

The mayor and police chief also outlined clear, achievable goals for YMP. These goals included reducing violence, restricting the availability of guns, and reaching the maximum number of youth in the city — those deemed at risk of involvement in violence, and others as well. The city also sought to engage the business community. For instance, the city has asked businesses to provide food to serve during mentoring sessions, or other items to use as rewards for youth participation. The mayor used his "publicity power" by speaking at the program kickoff, and continues to check in on progress.

Contact:

Gary J. Gemme, Chief of Police
Worcester Police Department
9-11 Lincoln Square
Worcester, MA 01608
(508) 868-8111
GemmeG@ci.worcester.ma.us

Resources

Partners on this Report

Office of Community Oriented Policing Services (COPS)
U.S. Department of Justice
1100 Vermont Avenue, N.W.
Washington, DC 20530
(202) 307-1480 or (800) 421-6770
www.cops.usdoj.gov

The COPS Office was created as a result of the Violent Crime Control and Law Enforcement Act of 1994. As a component of the Justice Department, the mission of the COPS Office is to advance community policing in jurisdictions of all sizes across the country. Community policing represents a shift from more traditional law enforcement in that it focuses on prevention of crime and the fear of crime on a very local basis. COPS provides grants to tribal, state, and local law enforcement agencies to hire and train community policing professionals, acquire and deploy cutting-edge crime-fighting technologies, and develop and test innovative policing strategies. COPS-funded training helps advance community policing at all levels of law enforcement — from line officers to law enforcement executives — as well as others in the criminal justice field. Because community policing is by definition inclusive, COPS training also reaches state and local government leaders and the citizens they serve. This broad range of programs helps COPS offer agencies support in virtually every aspect of law enforcement, and it is making America safer, one neighborhood at a time.

International Association of Chiefs of Police
515 North Washington Street
Alexandria, VA 22314
(703) 836-6767 (p)
(703) 836-4543 (f)
www.theiacp.org

IACP is the world's oldest and largest nonprofit membership organization of police executives. Through peer networking, publications, training, and advocacy for its members, IACP promotes ethical behavior, appreciation of diversity, community partnerships, technology use, research on youth and violent crime, and community safety programs.

Further Resources

American Probation and Parole Association (APPA)

P.O. Box 11910
Lexington, KY 40578
(859) 244-8203 (p)
(859) 244-8001 (f)
www.appa-net.org

APPA provides training and technical assistance, an information clearinghouse, and advocacy in the field of community-based corrections. APPA offers technical assistance to help develop and advance youth courts, as well as national and regional training for community corrections professionals. Publication topic areas include: community partnerships for restorative juvenile justice, probation and parole reform, and intensive supervision strategies for drug-involved offenders.

Brady Center to Prevent Gun Violence

1225 Eye Street, N.W.
Suite 1100
Washington, DC 20005
(202) 289-7319 (p)
(202) 408-1815 (f)
www.bradycenter.org

As the largest national, nonpartisan, grassroots organization leading the fight to prevent gun violence, the Brady Center is dedicating to creating an America free from gun violence. The Brady Center's Law Enforcement Relations (LER) Department works closely with law enforcement throughout the country, implementing programs to reduce gun violence in schools and communities, and providing research and education programs for law enforcement officers and parents.

Center for Community Safety (CCS)

500 West Fourth Street
Suite 102
Winston-Salem, NC 27102
(336) 750-3470 (p)
(336) 750-3480 (f)
www.centerforcommunitysafety.org

CCS is a community-based center of Winston-Salem State University that helps shape the way local communities respond to violence impacting residents, by spearheading the use of new approaches and drawing on new partnerships to address public safety issues in the Winston-Salem community. Developed through the Department of Justice Strategic Approaches to Community Safety Initiative, CCS plays a key role in national initiatives like Project Safe Neighborhoods and the Urban Institute's Reentry Mapping Network, and also manages the Weed and Seed initiative for Winston-Salem.

Centers for Disease Control and Prevention — National Center for Injury Prevention and Control

4770 Buford Highway NE
Atlanta, GA 30341
(800) 232-4636
www.cdc.gov/ncipc/factsheets/yvprevention.htm

This web site on youth violence prevention strategies links to fact sheets, resources, and organizations that can be helpful in planning youth violence prevention and education programs, including: the National Youth Violence Prevention Resource Center; the CDC's best practices sourcebook and school health guidelines; the Surgeon General's report on youth violence; and a compendium of assessment tools for youth violence.

Center for the Study and Prevention of Violence (CSPV)

1877 Broadway
Suite 601
Boulder, CO 80302
(303) 492-1032 (p)
(303) 443-3297 (f)
www.colorado.edu/cspv

CSPV provides informed assistance to groups committed to understanding and preventing violence, particularly adolescent violence, through a searchable virtual "Information House" stocked with research and resources, as well as technical assistance and data analysis for violence prevention programs. In Blueprints for Violence Prevention, CSPV identifies 11 effective violence prevention programs as models. CSVP's Safe Communities ~ Safe Schools Model enables educators, law enforcement, civic leaders, and community members to collaborate to design custom safe school plans.

Child Welfare League of America (CWLA)

440 First Street, N.W.
Third Floor
Washington, DC 20001-2085
(202) 638-2952 (p)
(202) 638-4004 (f)
www.cwla.org

CWLA is the nation's oldest and largest membership-based child welfare association, helping neighborhoods, communities, organizations, and governments work together to ensure that all children have the opportunity to grow up healthy and strong. CWLA's Juvenile Justice Division promotes juvenile justice system reform and community-based intervention and treatment alternatives, offering research, advocacy, training, and technical assistance programs.

Federal Youth Court Program

c/o National Council of Juvenile and Family Court Judges
P.O. Box 8970
Reno, NV 89507
(775) 784-6012 (p)
(775) 784-6628 (f)
www.youthcourt.net

As part of the Federal Youth Court Program, the National Council of Juvenile and Family Court Judges serves as a central point of contact for youth court programs across the nation, provides informational services, delivers training and technical assistance, and develops resource materials on how to develop and enhance youth court programs in the United States.

Fight Crime: Invest in Kids

1212 New York Avenue
Suite 300
Washington, DC 20005
(202) 776-0027 (p)
(202) 776-0110 (f)
www.fightcrime.org

Fight Crime: Invest in Kids is a national, bipartisan, nonprofit anti-crime organization of more than 3,000 police chiefs, sheriffs, prosecutors, other law enforcement leaders, and violence survivors. Fight Crime produces research on what keeps kids from becoming criminals, and puts that information in the hands of policymakers and the public. Reports include "Caught in the Crossfire: Arresting Gang Violence by Investing in Kids," and "Bullying Prevention is Crime Prevention."

Institute for Community Peace (ICP)

1522 K Street, N.W.
Suite 1100
Washington, DC 20005
(202) 393-7731 (p)
(202) 393-4148 (f)
www.instituteforcommunitypeace.org

ICP promotes a safe, healthy, and peaceful nation by mobilizing community resources and leadership to support strategies that emphasize civic empowerment. ICP partners with communities and facilitates their movement toward community peace and away from inaction over social problems through capacity-building technical assistance projects and trainings for community practitioners and policymakers.

National Association of School Resource Officers (NASRO)

1951 Woodlane Drive
St. Paul, MN 55125
(888) 316-2776 (p)
(651) 457-5665 (f)
www.nasro.org

NASRO is an organization for school based law enforcement officers, school administrators, and school security/safety professionals working as partners to protect students, school faculty and staff, and the schools they attend.

National Council on Crime and Delinquency (NCCD)

1970 Broadway
Suite 500
Oakland, CA 94612
(510) 208-0500 (p)
(510) 208-0511 (f)
www.nccd-crc.org

NCCD promotes effective, humane, fair, and economically sound solutions to family, community, and justice problems. Through research, reform initiatives, and work with individuals, public and private organizations, and the media, NCCD works to prevent and reduce crime and delinquency. Reforming Juvenile Justice Through

Comprehensive Community Planning is NCCD's implementation guide for a strategy that blends a strong prevention component with a system of graduated sanctions.

National Crime Prevention Council (NCPC)

1000 Connecticut Avenue, N.W.
13th Floor
Washington, DC 20036-5325
(202) 466-6272 (p)
(202) 296-1356 (f)
www.ncpc.org

NCPC enables people to create safer and more caring communities by addressing the causes of crime and violence and reducing the opportunities for crime to occur. NCPC's tools for community crime prevention include publications, teaching materials, community and school programs, trainings at the national, regional, and local levels, and public service announcements. NCPC has launched Prevention Works, a national blog featuring the latest news and ideas in crime prevention, and opportunities for discussion, available at: http://ncpc.typepad.com/prevention_works_blog/.

National Sheriffs' Association (NSA)

1450 Duke Street
Alexandria, VA 22314-3490
(703) 836-7827 (p)
(703) 683-6541 (f)
www.sheriffs.org

NSA is dedicated to raising the level of professionalism among those in the criminal justice field through professional development trainings, conferences, publications, advocacy, and an awards and scholarships program.

National School Safety Center (NSSC)

141 Duesenberg Drive
Suite 11
Westlake Village, CA 91362
(805) 373-9977 (p)
(805) 373-9277 (f)
www.schoolsafety.us

NSSC serves as an advocate for safe, secure, and peaceful schools worldwide and as a catalyst for the prevention of school crime and violence, by helping schools incorporate safety in their total academic plan. NSSC provides educators, law enforcers, and other youth-serving professionals with on-site technical assistance, school safety keynote addresses, training in safe schools planning, expert witness and trial consultation, and school safety research, best practices, and trends.

National Youth Gang Center (NYGC)

Institute for Intergovernmental Research
P.O. Box 12729
Tallahassee, FL 32317
(850) 385-0600 (p)
(850) 386-5356 (f)
www.iir.com/nygc

NYGC is a component of the Office of Juvenile Justice and Delinquency Prevention's coordinated, comprehensive response to growing gang problems in large and small cities, small suburbs, and even rural areas over the last two decades. NYGC assesses the scope and characteristics of youth gang activity in the United States, develops resources and makes them available to the field, and provides training and technical assistance in support of community-based prevention, intervention, and suppression efforts, including a large set of publications available on NYGC's web site.

National Youth Violence Prevention Resource Center

P.O. Box 10809
Rockville, MD 20849-0809
(866) 723-3968 (p)
(888) 503-3952 (TTY)
(301) 562-1001 (f)
www.safeyouth.org

Developed as a gateway for law enforcement, educators, community organizers, parents, and youth, the National Youth Violence Prevention Resource Center provides current information developed by federal agencies or with federal support, including the latest tools to facilitate discussion with children, to resolve conflicts nonviolently, to stop bullying, to prevent teen suicide, and to end violence committed by and against young people. Resources include fact sheets, best practices documents, funding and conference announcements, statistics, research bulletins, and surveillance reports.

Office for Victims of Crime (OVC)

U.S. Department of Justice
810 Seventh Street, NW
Eighth Floor
Washington, DC 20531
To order publications: (800) 851-3420/ TTY (877) 712-9279
For training or technical assistance information: (866) 682-8822
www.ovc.gov

OVC oversees diverse programs that benefit victims of crime, providing funding to state victim assistance and compensation programs, and supporting trainings that educate criminal justice and allied professionals about the rights and needs of crime victims.

Office of Juvenile Justice and Delinquency Prevention (OJJDP) — Truancy Prevention

U.S. Department of Justice
810 Seventh Street, N.W.
Washington, DC 20531
(202) 307-5911
www.ojjdp.ncjrs.org/truancy

OJJDP, in partnership with the Office of Safe and Drug-Free Schools, has developed a web site to collect and disseminate truancy-related information and resources. The site's resources focus on preventing truancy through partnerships among educators, law enforcement, courts, communities, and families.

Police Executive Research Forum (PERF)

1120 Connecticut Avenue, N.W.
Suite 930
Washington, DC 20036
(202) 466-7820 (p)
(202) 466-7826 (f)
www.policeforum.org

PERF is a national membership organization of progressive police executives from the largest city, county, and state law enforcement agencies. PERF works to improve policing and advance professionalism through research and involvement in public policy debate. PERF's Training and Technical Assistance Division provides community policing training and technical assistance to law enforcement agencies and communities, and has developed a self-assessment tool for law enforcement agencies to gauge their level of community policing implementation.

Prevention Institute UNITY Project

265 29th Street
Oakland, CA 94611
Contact Lissette Flores at (510) 444-7738 ext. 324 (p)
(510) 663-1280 (f)
www.preventioninstitute.org/UNITY.html

UNITY (Urban Networks to Increase Thriving Youth Through Violence
Prevention), a CDC funded partnership between the Prevention Institute and public
health/injury prevention researchers from Harvard and UCLA, aims to engage youth
and representatives of the 45 largest cities, along with national violence prevention
advocates and leaders, in a National Consortium to shape the U.S. strategy for urban
youth violence prevention. UNITY provides tools, training, and technical assistance to
help cities be more effective in preventing youth violence.

PRIDE Youth Programs

4 West Oak Street
Fremont, MI 49412
(231) 924-1662 (p)
(231) 924-5663 (f)
www.prideyouthprograms.org

PRIDE is the nation's oldest and largest peer-to-peer organization devoted to
prevention of drug abuse and violence through education. PRIDE hosts the world's
largest youth drug and violence prevention conference each year, bringing together
local, national, and international organizations. PRIDE Youth Teams reach students
and communities through schools, civic organizations, and drug task forces, using
creative outlets like song and dance to emphasize community service, drug education,
and drug-free activities.

Street Law, Inc.

101 Wayne Avenue
Suite 870
Silver Spring, MD 20910
(301) 589-1130 (p)
(301) 589-1131 (f)
www.streetlaw.org

Street Law creates youth programs and curricula to increase the effective teaching
of law, democracy, and human rights through practical, participatory education.
Street Law promotes the knowledge of legal rights and responsibilities and engage-

ment in the democratic process, as well as cooperative learning and critical thinking. Street Law for school resource officers is a curriculum that develops positive interaction between students and school resource officers, through group discussions and hands-on activities exploring the roles and responsibilities of both police officers and members of the community.

Teens, Crime, and the Community (TCC)
1000 Connecticut Avenue, NW
13th Floor
Washington, DC 20036-5325
(202) 261-4161 (p)
(202) 296-1356 (f)
www.nationaltcc.org

TCC helps teens understand how crime affects them and their families, friends, and communities, and involves them in crime prevention projects that make communities safer and more vital. The comprehensive Community Works curriculum guides schools, police officers, and other community partners in creating law-related violence and crime prevention programming. Through Youth Safety Corps, a club model, youth partner with school resource officers and other community adults to assess needs and implement programs that address physical and social safety issues in their schools and communities.

Youth Crime Watch of America (YCWA)
9200 South Dadeland Boulevard
Suite 417
Miami, FL 33156
(305) 670-2409 (p)
(305) 670-3805 (f)
www.ycwa.org

YCWA brings youth of all backgrounds together to identify and correct problems unique to their schools and communities, teaching and encouraging crime reporting, school patrols, youth-youth mentoring, conflict resolution, and other crime prevention strategies. Youth take ownership for their own programs in schools, neighborhoods, public housing sites, recreation centers, or parks.

About This Report

Under a cooperative agreement by the U.S. Department of Justice Office of Community Oriented Policing Services, NLC's Institute for Youth, Education, and Families (YEF Institute) began an effort in the fall of 2005 to identify and highlight partnerships between mayors and law enforcement leaders that promote the safety and well-being of children and youth.

Drawing upon the advice and support of the International Association of Chiefs of Police and a new NLC Advisory Group on Mayor-Law Enforcement Partnerships, the YEF Institute initially reviewed more than 30 city initiatives addressing issues such as youth violence, bullying, delinquency prevention, and substance abuse. Phone interviews with city and police officials conducted during the first half of 2006, supplemented in many instances by written descriptions submitted by these local leaders, provided the basis for detailed profiles of each city-based effort. The advisory group met in November 2005 to help frame the project's research design and reconvened in June 2006 to review and cull key lessons from the city summaries prepared by YEF Institute staff.

The criteria that guided final selection of city examples for the report included evidence of strong mayor-law enforcement collaboration, impact, and sustainability over time. The resulting profiles of mayor-law enforcement partnerships reflect the diversity of America's cities and towns, drawn from nearly every region of the nation and from communities both large and small. The report provides an in-depth look at innovative strategies utilized in seven cities: Boston, Massachusetts; Burnsville, Minnesota; El Paso, Texas; New Brighton, Minnesota; New Haven, Connecticut; Sallisaw, Oklahoma; and San José, California. Profiles from 10 other communities offer additional insights into possible approaches to collaboration between police departments and other city agencies.

This project was supported by cooperative agreement #2005HSWXK013 by the Office of Community Oriented Policing Services, U.S. Department of Justice. The opinions contained herein are those of the authors and do not necessarily represent the official position of the U.S. Department of Justice. References to specific companies, products, or services should not be considered an endorsement of the product by the author or the U.S. Department of Justice. Rather, the references are illustrations to supplement discussion of the issues.

www.ingramcontent.com/pod-product-compliance
Lightning Source LLC
Chambersburg PA
CBHW080852010626
R18376000001B/R183760PG45790CBX00015B/3